baby einstein.

D0501810

The ABCs of ART
A–M

The WALT DISNEP Company

Fine Art Credits:
Angel Annunciating, by Lorenzo Lotto (1480–1556), transparency, Reunion des Musees Nationaux/Art Resource, New York • *Roter Ballon*, by Paul Klee (1879–1940), Artist Rights Society (ARS), New York; VG Bild-Kunst, Bonn, transparency, Girandon/Art Resource, New York • *Cows*, by Vincent van Gogh (1853–1890), transparency, Girandon/Art Resource, New York • *Young Boy with Dog*, by Pablo Picasso (1881–1973), Estate of Pablo Picasso/Artist Rights Society (ARS), New York, transparency, Scala/Art Resource, New York • *African Elephants*, by Charles-Emile Vacher de Tournemine (1812–1872), transparency, Girandon/Art Resource, New York • *Flag on an Orange Field*, by Jasper Johns (b. 1930), Jasper Johns/licensed by VAGA, transparency, Girandon/Art Resource, New York • *Reading (La Lecture)*, by Auguste Renoir (1841–1919), transparency, Reunion des Musees Nationaux/Art Resource, New York • *Little Blue Horse*, by Franz Marc (1880–1916), transparency, Girandon/Art Resource, New York • *Untitled (ice cream)*, by Andy Warhol (1928–1987), The Andy Warhol Foundation for the Visual Arts/Artist Rights Society (ARS), New York, transparency, The Andy Warhol Foundation, Inc./Art Resource, New York • *Monkidew*, by Kenny Scharf (b. 1958), Kenny Scharf/Artist Rights Society (ARS), New York, transparency, Art Resource, New York • *Untitled (kite)*, by Andy Warhol (1928–1987), The Andy Warhol Foundation for the Visual Arts/Artist Rights Society (ARS), New York, transparency, The Andy Warhol Foundation, Inc./Art Resource, New York • *Lion at Rest*, by Rembrandt van Rijn (1606–1669), transparency, Girandon/Art Resource, New York • *Sueno (Dream)*, by Alfredo Arreguin (b. 1935), Smithsonian Art Museum, Washington D.C./Art Resource, New York

Hyperion Books for Children, New York
Copyright © 2004 by The Baby Einstein Company, LLC.
All Rights Reserved.
Baby Einstein and the Boy's Head Logo are trademarks of The Baby Einstein Company, LLC. All Rights Reserved.
EINSTEIN and ALBERT EINSTEIN are trademarks of The Hebrew University of Jerusalem. All Rights Reserved.
For information address Hyperion Books for Children, 114 Fifth Avenue, New York, New York 10011-5690.
Printed in China
Library of Congress Cataloging Card Number on file.
ISBN 0-7868-3807-8

Visit www.hyperionbooksforchildren.com and www.babyeinstein.com

Great Minds Start Little.™

Aa

angel

A **is for angel.**

Look carefully.

What is the angel holding?

What makes this angel different from you?

Bb

balloon

B **is for balloon.**

Point to the balloon in the painting. What color is it?

The balloon is a circle shape. What other shapes do you see?

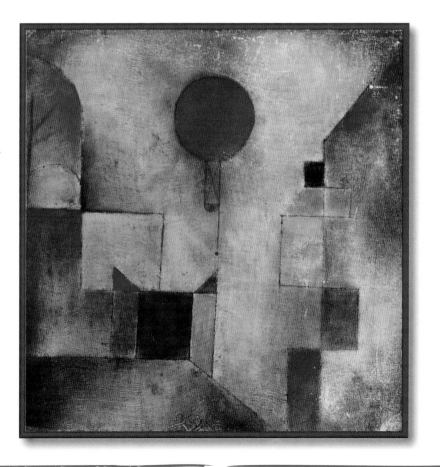

Cc

COWS

C is for cows.

Do you think it is spring, summer, fall, or winter in this painting?

What does the artist use more: curvy lines or straight lines?

Dd

dog

D is for dog.

What color does the artist use most in this painting?

What do you imagine the person and the dog are looking at?

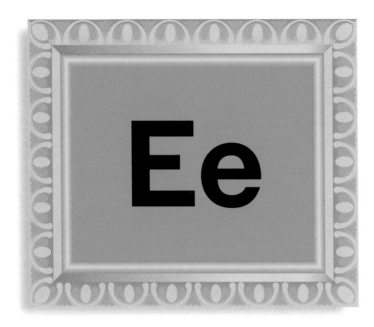

elephants

E is for elephants.

What time of day do you think it is in this painting?

If you were in this scene, what sounds might you hear?

Ff

flag

F is for flag.

What colors are in the American flag?

What shapes do you see in this painting?

Gg

girls

_G_ is for girls.

How do you think these girls know each other? Do you think they're sisters? Friends?

What do you think would be nice names for these girls?

Hh

horse

H **is for horse.**

Name five colors that you see in this painting.

Can you find mountains in the scene?

ice cream

I is for ice cream.

What shape is the cone?
What shape is the ice cream?

Which two shades of color in
the artwork are the most alike?

I i

jungle

J is for jungle.

Look carefully. Can you find two snakes?

If you could enter this painting, what would the scene smell like? Sound like? Feel like?

Kk

kite

K is for kite.

What is it that keeps the kite from flying away?

Point to two things that are blue.

Ll

lion

L is for lion.

What two colors are in this drawing?

How do you think this lion is feeling? Sleepy? Angry? Hungry?

monkeys

M **is for monkeys.**

How many monkeys do you see in this painting?

Where do you think these monkeys live?